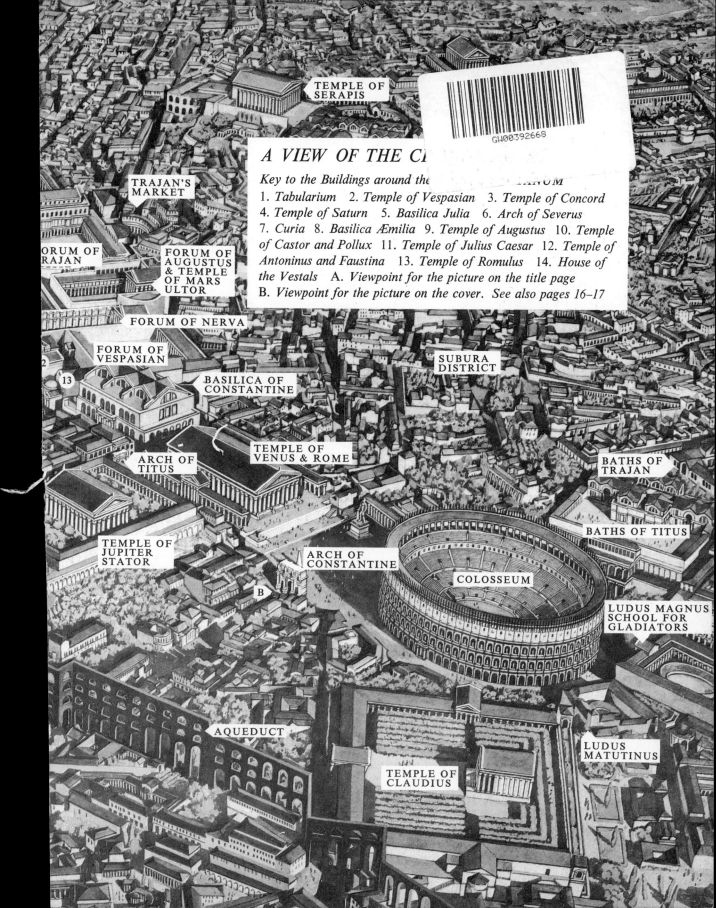

TEMPLE OF SERAPIS

TRAJAN'S MARKET

FORUM OF TRAJAN

FORUM OF AUGUSTUS & TEMPLE OF MARS ULTOR

FORUM OF NERVA

FORUM OF VESPASIAN

13

BASILICA OF CONSTANTINE

SUBURA DISTRICT

ARCH OF TITUS

TEMPLE OF VENUS & ROME

BATHS OF TRAJAN

BATHS OF TITUS

TEMPLE OF JUPITER STATOR

ARCH OF CONSTANTINE

B

COLOSSEUM

LUDUS MAGNUS SCHOOL FOR GLADIATORS

AQUEDUCT

TEMPLE OF CLAUDIUS

LUDUS MATUTINUS

*A VIEW OF THE CI...*

*Key to the Buildings around the* ...NUM

*1. Tabularium  2. Temple of Vespasian  3. Temple of Concord*
*4. Temple of Saturn  5. Basilica Julia  6. Arch of Severus*
*7. Curia  8. Basilica Æmilia  9. Temple of Augustus  10. Temple*
*of Castor and Pollux  11. Temple of Julius Caesar  12. Temple of*
*Antoninus and Faustina  13. Temple of Romulus  14. House of*
*the Vestals  A. Viewpoint for the picture on the title page*
*B. Viewpoint for the picture on the cover.  See also pages 16–17*

GW00392668

*Dena Crouch*
*5/2/83*

*Also by Helen and Richard Leacroft*

THE BUILDINGS OF ANCIENT MAN
THE BUILDINGS OF ANCIENT EGYPT
·THE BUILDINGS OF ANCIENT GREECE
THE BUILDINGS OF ANCIENT MESOPOTAMIA

*In preparation*

THE BUILDINGS OF ANCIENT ISLAM
THE BUILDINGS OF BYZANTIUM

Richard Leacroft trained as an architect and
scene designer, and is now Head of the Department
of Preliminary Studies in the School of Architecture,
Leicester College of Art. Helen Leacroft trained
as an actress at RADA, but later turned to teaching,
and now specializes in History and Scripture.

Copyright © 1969 by Helen and Richard Leacroft
First published 1969 jointly by Brockhampton Press Ltd, Leicester
(now Hodder & Stoughton Children's Books) and Young Scott Books,
a Division of the Addison-Wesley Publishing Company, Inc., Reading,
Massachusetts 01867, USA.
Third impression 1975
UK ISBN 0 340 04205 2
USA ISBN 0 201 09145 3

Library of Congress Catalog Card No. 69-18971.
Printed and bound in Great Britain by
Morrison & Gibb Ltd, London and Edinburgh.

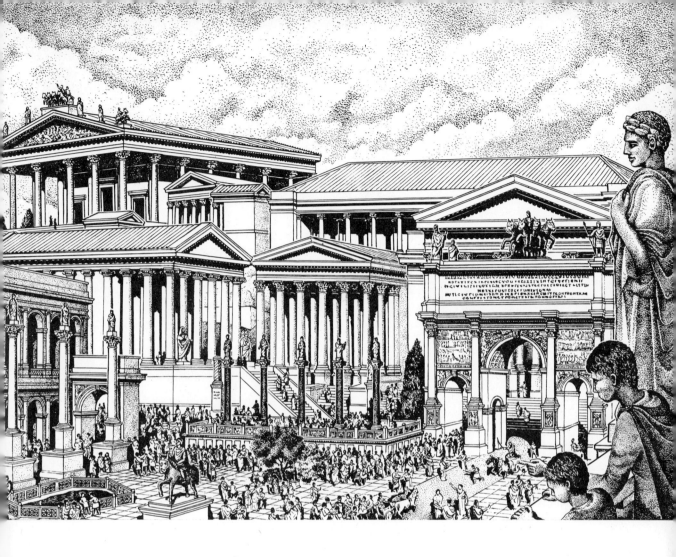

# THE BUILDINGS OF
# ANCIENT ROME

## Helen and Richard Leacroft

HODDER & STOUGHTON
LONDON  LEICESTER  SYDNEY  AUCKLAND
*and*
ADDISON-WESLEY PUBLISHING COMPANY

*VILLAGE HUT, 8th cent. B.C. from the primitive village on the Palatine, Rome*

*ETRUSCAN TOMB, Tarquinii, burial ceremony, 5th cent. B.C.*

*In the second century A.D. the great Empire of Rome was at its height. Throughout the Mediterranean lands, into Asia, and across Europe as far north as Britain, a network of roads spread out along which the Roman legions marched keeping the Pax Romana, the peace of Rome. Many of the conquered peoples were often ready to adopt Roman ways of life, and the Romans themselves adapted and copied from those with whom they came in contact. In this way their civilization spread and developed, and so it is not only in Rome itself that we must look for evidence of her buildings, but throughout the whole Empire.*

*Roman society was more complicated than that of the Greeks, and many new types of buildings were needed to house its wide range of activities. New building methods were introduced, and it is mainly through the use of the arch, the vault and the dome, on a scale made possible by their invention of concrete, that the Romans were able to develop the necessary buildings.*

*The city of Rome, founded according to legend by Romulus, developed in the eighth century B.C. from a number of individual villages set on seven hills, protected on the east by the Alban hills, and on the north by the fast-flowing Tiber. The forum or market-place was in the valley, and here the people from the villages met together for religious ceremonies, political meetings and trade.*

# THE ETRUSCANS AND EARLY ROME

*ARCH OF AUGUSTUS, PERUGIA, 3rd cent. B.C.*

In the twelfth century B.C. peoples from the Aegean lands settled to the north of the Tiber in the area called Etruria. Although few traces of Etruscan cities remain, their tombs are still to be seen. Many of these were built to look like their homes, for these people believed that life on earth and life after death were much the same, so their tombs were houses and were often painted with frescoes of daily life. Many Roman houses followed this pattern, with smoke-holes in the roof (page 34), and it was from the Etruscans that the Romans learned the art of building a true arch made up of wedge-shaped stones—voussoirs—fitting closely into a perfect semi-circle.

The Etruscans built temples where their gods could be worshipped. Unlike Greek temples which had steps all round, these had steps at the front only, set between flanking walls. They led up to a platform—*podium**—across which was a deep portico. The earliest temples of Etruria and Rome were generally built of timber and sun-dried mud-brick. Tiles of terracotta—baked clay—covered the roof-rafters, and the ends of the timber beams were protected by decorated terracotta slabs. The roof projected over the side walls to form large eaves which protected the mud-bricks from the dripping rain-water. Although some temples contained only one room—*cella*, others were divided into three, each room being dedicated to a different god.

\* Throughout this book Latin words in the text are printed in italic type.

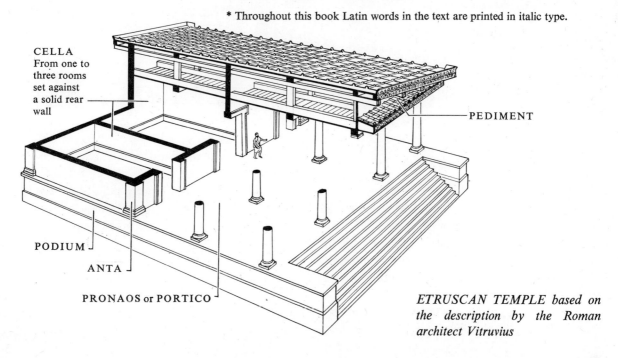

CELLA
From one to three rooms set against a solid rear wall

PEDIMENT

PODIUM

ANTA

PRONAOS or PORTICO

*ETRUSCAN TEMPLE based on the description by the Roman architect Vitruvius*

3

# ROMAN TEMPLES

By the first century A.D. the Roman temple had developed into the type of building seen above. It was built within a sacred area—temenos, around which was a covered walking way or colonnade—peribolos, or at one end of a public *forum*. Before the temple stood an altar where sacrifices were offered and soothsayers—*haruspices*—interpreted the omens by examining the insides of sacrificial animals and birds, to find out if good fortune would attend civic or private enterprises.

Many Roman temples were built like those of the Greeks with an open colonnade all round (pages 6, 8, 9), but the type most usually found developed from the Etruscan temple, with a single *cella* inside and with the surrounding columns attached to the side walls (as above) in place of the open colonnade. There was a deep portico at the front, and the whole building was raised on a high *podium* approached by steps at

4

the front set between two flanking walls, although in some cases when the front of the *podium* was to be used by orators the steps would be at the sides. In the example shown above, based on the Maison Carrée at Nîmes, the colonnades surrounding the temenos have been shown as being built in the Doric order, whilst the Corinthian order, with its decorative capitals of acanthus leaves, is used on the temple itself. The Ionic order with its spiral volutes was also used, and a combination of the

Corinthian and Ionic called the Composite.

The interiors of the temples were decorated with coloured marbles, with niches containing statues set between flat pilasters or columns attached to the walls. The *cella* ceiling was either flat with rectangular timber panels or coffers, or sometimes barrel-vaulted (page 11) in stone or concrete. In many cases the statue of the god was placed on a raised platform at the end of the *cella*, approached by steps, and sometimes set in a semi-circular apse.

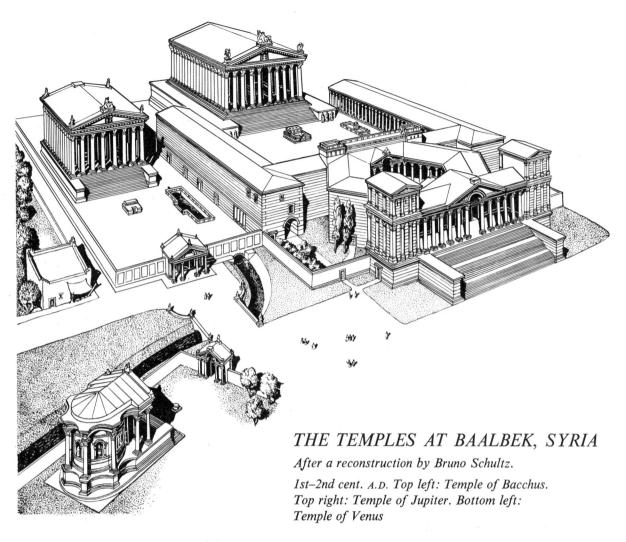

*THE TEMPLES AT BAALBEK, SYRIA*

*After a reconstruction by Bruno Schultz.*

*1st–2nd cent.* A.D. *Top left: Temple of Bacchus.*
*Top right: Temple of Jupiter. Bottom left:*
*Temple of Venus*

The Romans believed that everything in their lives was controlled by the gods. The State provided the temples where the sacred rites were performed; and when countries were conquered temples were erected so that the worship of the gods could continue there. The imposing buildings also kept the idea of the might of Rome before the conquered peoples. Such a temple group was built at Baalbek in Syria.

The Romans also built circular temples, often with a small entrance portico, such as may be seen above. The circular temple of Vesta in the *Forum Romanum* was the most sacred shrine in the city, for it was here that the Vestal Virgins attended the sacred hearth fire which was always kept burning. As the Empire grew and spoils were collected they were placed in the temples which became State treasuries. Ordinary people were also allowed to deposit their valuables for safe keeping, but they did not enter the temples for worship.

There were two types of deities: those who were concerned with the care and

## THE TEMPLE OF MITHRAS

*Carrawburgh, Northumberland,
Britain, 3rd–4th cent. A.D.*

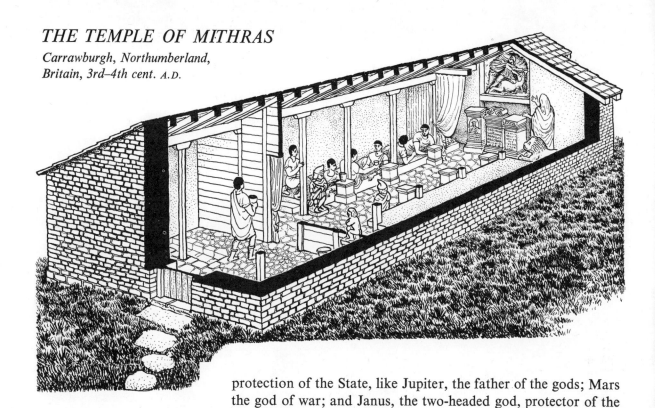

*TEMPLE OF PORTUNUS,
ROME, 1st cent. A.D.
Earlier known as the
Temple of Vesta*

protection of the State, like Jupiter, the father of the gods; Mars the god of war; and Janus, the two-headed god, protector of the gates. In later times the Emperor was also worshipped as a god. The more personal gods were those of the household. Daily offerings were made in the home to the *penates*, the guardians of the hearth, and every house of substance had its own *lararium* or shrine (page 36, caption 9) to the *lares familiares*, the spirits which protected the household, and here the head of the family—*pater familias*—offered libations.

As well as acknowledging their own native gods some Romans followed the mystery cults of the East; from contact with Egypt came the cult of Isis, the mother-goddess of the earth. Wherever Roman soldiers were stationed the worship of Mithras was found, for the god of light whose beginnings were in Persia became the protecting deity of the army. The *Mithraeum*, or sacred place, was originally a cave, an underground chamber or even a room in a house which was shut off from the light, and represented the cave in which the god was supposed to have been born. On each side of the long shrine were low benches on which the worshippers reclined to take part in the ritual banquet. At the end was an altar, the top of which was hollowed to take a lamp, and either on the front of the altar or on the wall behind it was a carving showing a representation of Mithras slaying a bull, from which all life-blood was thought to have come.

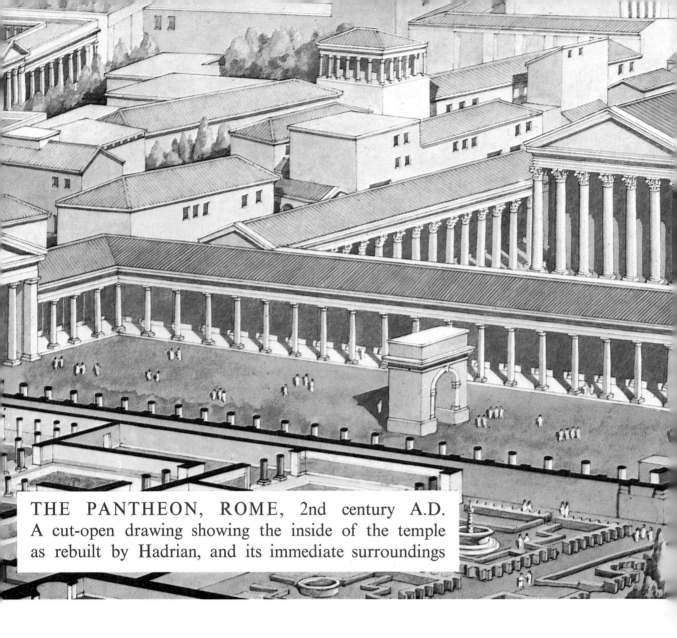

THE PANTHEON, ROME, 2nd century A.D.
A cut-open drawing showing the inside of the temple
as rebuilt by Hadrian, and its immediate surroundings

The Pantheon in Rome was the greatest and most perfect of the circular temples. The original building was erected by the son-in-law of Augustus, Agrippa, who was also responsible for the baths which lay to the south of the temple. Both baths and temple were rebuilt by the Emperor Hadrian between A.D. 118 and 128, but he repeated the original inscription which tells us that Marcus Agrippa, son of Lucius, Consul for the third time, built this. An inscription on the architrave shows that restoration was also carried out in the third century A.D. It is, however, possible to date the main building of the rotunda or round hall to Hadrian because many of the bricks used were stamped with dates varying between A.D. 125 and 128.

Standing at one end of a large colonnaded courtyard, the Pantheon was unlike the majority of Roman temples in that the *cella*, behind a normal columned portico, was built as a great circular room over one hundred and forty feet across. The word pantheon, meaning 'all gods',

indicates the purpose of the building, which differed from the majority of temples in being dedicated to seven gods. Around the circular walls were recesses for the statues of the gods, the places of honour being reserved for Mars and Venus, the protecting deities of Agrippa's family. The floor was paved with coloured marbles, as were the walls which supported the dome, at the top of which was a great circular *oculus*, an opening to the sky which provided all the light for the interior. The outside of the dome was

stepped in its lower levels, and the whole was originally covered with bronze sheeting which was replaced by lead in the eighth century A.D.

In A.D. 608 the Emperor Phocas presented the temple to the Pope, when it was re-dedicated as a Christian church, and has been used for this purpose ever since. Numerous alterations have been made to the interior, notably in the re-decoration of the upper part of the walls, where one bay has now been restored to the original design as shown in the drawing above.

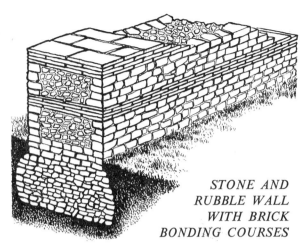

*STONE AND RUBBLE WALL WITH BRICK BONDING COURSES*

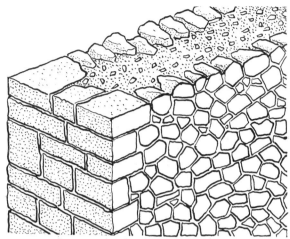

*WALL OF OPUS INCERTUM*

# MATERIALS AND CONSTRUCTION

Many different materials and methods were used. The early structures on the Palatine (page 2) were of mud-brick and wood, but the wet winters made more durable materials necessary, so walls were built with rough stones, rubble and clay set between solid stone facings. At first tufa was used, but it crumbled in the frost, so peperino, a volcanic rock which weathered well, took its place. From the first century B.C. travertine, a hard limestone, was employed.

From earliest times the builders had used lime mortar to bind the stones, but by adding volcanic dust they made pozzalano which, when mixed with sand and gravel and poured over the inner core of stones and rubble, set into solid concrete. Courses of bricks laid at intervals were used to bind the wall, and it was soon found that it was no longer necessary to build carefully dressed outer stone facings; instead irregularly shaped stones of different sizes were used. This method was known as *opus incertum*. Later square-based pyramids of stone were inserted with the points facing inwards, the square bases making a rectangular pattern on the surface of the wall; this was called *opus reticulatum*. A further development was the use of specially

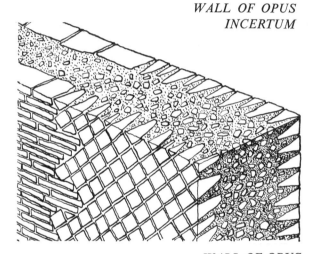

*WALL OF OPUS RETICULATUM*

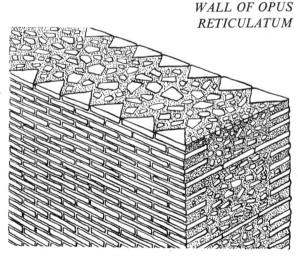

*WALL OF OPUS TESTACEUM*

10

*STABIAN BATHS, POMPEII. Dressing-room*

made triangular baked bricks—*opus testaceum*. The outer walls were usually covered with stucco, which was often painted, and marble slabs or stucco faced the inner walls so that the structural features that we see today were never in view. Public monuments were built of carefully cut stone masonry with iron clamps leaded into the joints to protect the structure from earthquakes. When used with concrete the masonry was often no more than a box facing.

It was the use of concrete which enabled an important feature of Roman architecture to develop, namely the use of arches and vaults. Concrete could be poured on to timber formwork and it set into a continuous solid mass. The earliest form of vault was the semi-circular tunnel or barrel-vault built off two continuous parallel walls. When a square was to be covered, two barrel-vaults were built at right angles crossing each other and forming a groin-vault. Several such cross-vaults could be used down the length of a building dividing the area into bays, the open side arches at the upper levels admitting light, as may be seen in the Market of Trajan, or fitted with windows as in the Basilica of Constantine (page 20). Half-domes and domes covered semi-circular and circular areas, and in Nero's *Domus Aurea* the architects found that by using concrete they could put a dome over an octagonal room.

*TRAJAN'S MARKET, ROME, 2nd cent. A.D.*
*The great hall with galleries and shops*

*THE DOMUS AUREA, ROME, 1st cent. A.D.*
*The domed octagonal hall of the great*
*House of Gold built for Nero*

The Roman love of order is well shown in the organization of great building projects. Brick and concrete construction made it essential for all the materials, some of which had to be transported from a distance, to be available at the required time. A law of Rome forbade any carts carrying goods from passing through the narrow streets during the day, the only exception being those of the building constructors. Brickworkers, carpenters, and marble workers were only a few of the craftsmen needed.

In the construction of the Pantheon, shown above, the walls were of brick-faced concrete; in the lower levels, where great strength was needed, the concrete contained alternate layers of lumps of travertine and tufa, and as they rose and needed lightening the travertine was replaced by broken brick. Liquid concrete was poured between the triangular-shaped bricks which were built up on both faces of the wall. At intervals horizontal courses of *bipedales*—bricks measuring two Roman feet ($23\frac{1}{4}$ in. or

59 cm.) square—were laid to bond the walls. Timber scaffolding was set up to provide ramps for the workers, and the Roman architect, Vitruvius, first century B.C., described a wooden crane that was in use. The arches were built with brick outer rings, and further bricks made compartments into which the concrete could be poured. Bricks were also laid flat on the timber formwork and remained as a facing when this was removed, so that the underside of arches and the face of walls were the same material,

and could be continuously covered with stucco.

The concrete of the upper part of the dome had to be as light as possible, so pumice was mixed with the tufa. To reduce the amount of concrete the ceiling was coffered, these sunken panels being built up in reverse on the wooden formwork on which the concrete for the dome was poured. To complete the dome the upper formwork would most probably have been supported on beams spanning from a central scaffold tower to the outer works.

13

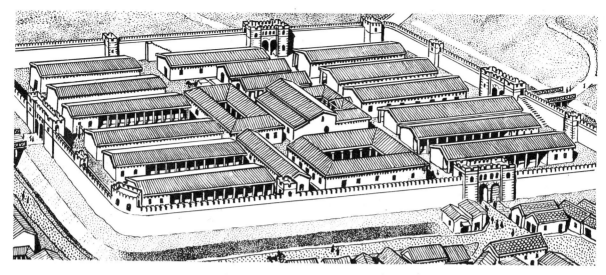

*HOUSESTEADS, Britain. Fort on the Roman Wall, 2nd–4th cent.* A.D.

# TOWNS

In Italy many early towns grew up in a natural way following the contours of the land, but in the provinces many towns grew out of or around the military forts and camps—*castrae*. These forts were rectangular in plan with rounded corners. In the middle was the headquarters building—*principia*, and adjoining this the commandant's house—*praetorium*—and bathhouse, and the granaries —*horrea*. The remainder of the space was allotted to barracks, stables and a hospital. Outside the walls were the homes of the army's local dependants and others seeking the protection of the garrison.

*Coloniae* were towns built for the settlement of Roman citizens, and land was granted to those men who had retired from the legions, who would be loyal to

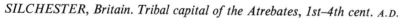

*SILCHESTER, Britain. Tribal capital of the Atrebates, 1st–4th cent.* A.D.

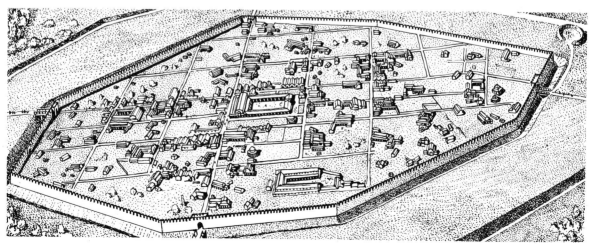

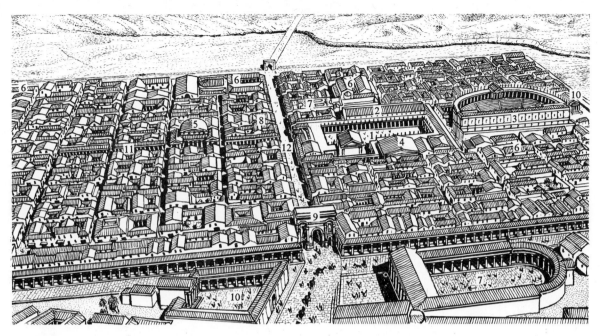

*TIMGAD, Algeria, 2nd cent. A.D.*

 1. *Forum*
 2. *Town hall*
 3. *Theatre, with shrine;*
    *see page 27*
 4. *Senate house*
 5. *Library*
 6. *Baths*
 7. *Markets*
 8. *Latrines*
 9. *Triumphal arch*
10. *Temples*
11. *Cardo: north–south street*
12. *Decumanus: east–west street*

Rome and would form a group who could hold office, organize defence, and supervise the building of the town. Surveyors from the army laid out the ground plan on the lines of an army camp, but here the headquarters buildings were replaced by the *forum* and public buildings. Some towns were created for the re-settlement of local tribes who were moved from their defensive areas to sites where they could be more readily controlled. In other instances a new town grew up on the existing tribal site.

Both camps and towns were laid out on a grid-iron plan. Originally two main roads connected the four gates in the protecting walls, and crossed each other at right angles. In the town the north–south road was the *cardo*, the east–west road the *decumanus*, both of which were sometimes lined with colonnades where shade and shelter were needed, as at Timgad in Algeria, and Palmyra in Syria. Lesser roads ran parallel to these enclosing a series of rectangular sites or islands—*insulae*. The Roman town had many public buildings. Around the central *forum* were to be found the *basilica* or law court; the *curia*, where the governing body met, and the temples to the gods. Although the majority of *insulae* had houses on them, others provided space for the theatre, the library and for baths and markets. The main streets and *fora* were often decorated with great triumphal arches to commemorate the victory of an emperor (see cover).

By the fourth century A.D., Rome itself had developed from its simple beginnings into a large city. Here there was no overall planning, but the main roads leading from the various *fora* wound their ways to the city gates. An aerial view of the central part of the city can be seen on the following pages.

PANTHEON

THEATRE
OF POMPEY

THEATRE OF
MARCELLUS

THE CAPITOL

FORUM
ROMANUM

TIBER

TEMPLE OF
PORTUNUS

THE PALATINE

CIRCUS
MAXIMUS

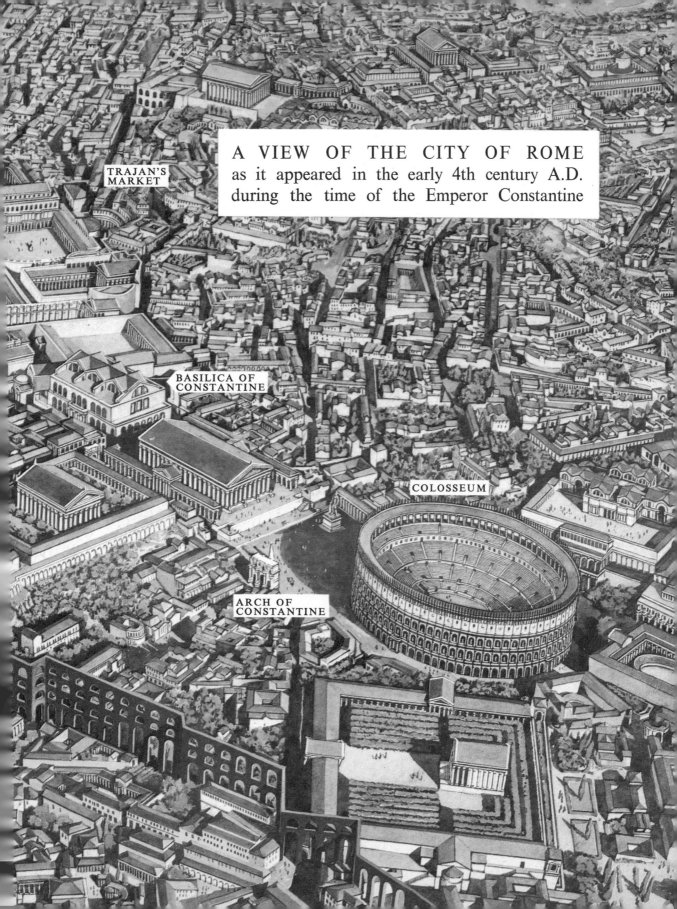

A VIEW OF THE CITY OF ROME as it appeared in the early 4th century A.D. during the time of the Emperor Constantine

TRAJAN'S MARKET

BASILICA OF CONSTANTINE

COLOSSEUM

ARCH OF CONSTANTINE

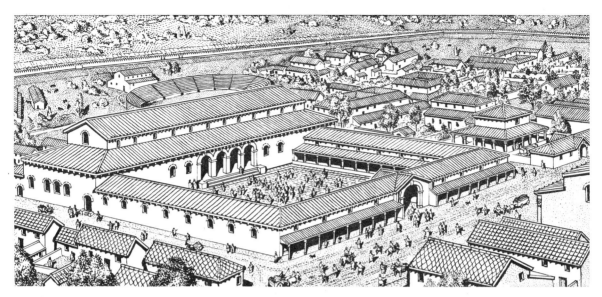

*BASILICA AND FORUM, Caerwent, Britain, 1st–4th cent.* A.D.

# POLITICS AND COMMERCE

The *forum* was an open square usually surrounded by colonnades. Here patricians—members of the nobility—met in the morning to discuss affairs of state and to further their business interests, for the quarters of the bankers and money-lenders were also to be found around this area. As Rome grew the farmers and tradesmen who had earlier used the *forum* as a market-place were banished to quarters which were specially built for them (page 11), and the *forum* was used for religious festivals, triumphal processions and public meetings. The emperors, however, soon realized that the *Forum Romanum* (see title page) was too small for the growing population and they therefore built further *fora*. In provincial cities the traders' quarters were set as close to the *forum* as possible. In many instances the shops opened on to the colonnades of the *forum* or faced outwards on to the main street, as at Caerwent. These shops, following the Roman pattern, were open at the front, a counter stretching across the opening, with a gap at one end through which the shopkeeper could enter his premises. At the back of the shop, stairs, or sometimes a wooden ladder, led to an upper room which was used as living quarters. When the shop was closed, wooden shutters, which fitted into grooves at top and bottom, were placed in position over the front opening.

Traders concerned with certain types of goods usually had their premises close to each other; for they were organized in guilds or corporations which were responsible for controlling the quality of the goods which their members sold. Under the arcades around the traders' *forum* behind the theatre at Ostia, there were offices with mosaic floors in front of them which illustrated the trade of the owners, caulkers, furriers, corn merchants, fitters; set in the mosaics were their names and pictures of their ships, and the places they traded with, such as Sabratha on the North African coast with its elephants.

All Roman citizens, whether patricians or the ordinary people—*plebs*, and those freemen who lived in the Empire under Roman rule, were entitled to justice. This was administered by magistrates in the *basilica*. The earliest basilicas were divided inside by rows of columns into a central nave and side aisles. The columns supported an upper wall with windows and the timber and tiled pitched roof; the width of the nave being determined by the lengths of timber available for the roof-trusses. This type of construction continued in use throughout the whole Roman period in places where the weather made a pitched roof desirable, as at Caerwent in Britain where the high nave may be seen flanked by the lower aisles.

The magistrates' tribunal, with seats for the assessors and the *praetor* and an altar for sacrifices, was on a raised dais inside a semi-circular apse, or a rectangular recess, and was usually placed opposite the entrance, which was either at one end or in the middle of a side wall. Interested spectators gathered in the nave or the galleries at first-floor level to listen to the proceedings.

The use of concrete for vaults and cross-vaults changed the shape and appearance of the basilicas, and the columns down the length of the building were no longer needed. The walls were richly decorated with coloured marbles and statues were placed in niches, as may be seen in the *basilica* of Constantine (page 20). Many basilicas were later adapted and used as Christian churches.

*FORUM AND BASILICA OF SEPTIMUS SEVERUS, Leptis Magna, Tripolitania, 3rd cent. A.D.*

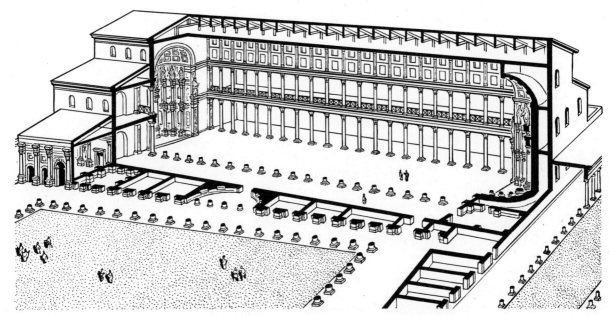

## THE BASILICA OF MAXENTIUS AND CONSTANTINE

*Rome, circa* A.D. 300

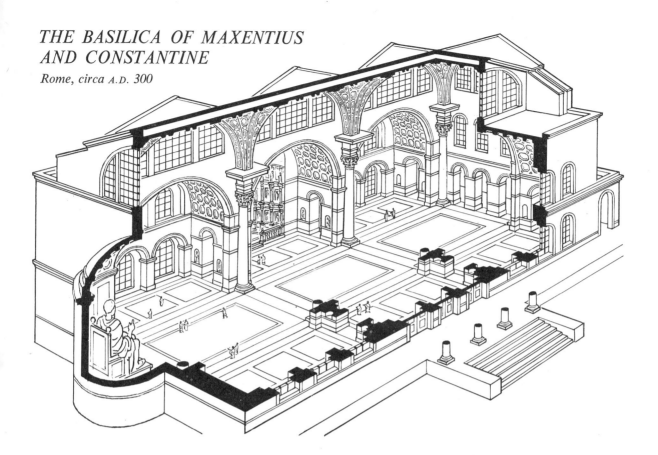

The spread of the Empire led to the growth of trade; foodstuffs, wines, oil, spices and goods of all descriptions poured into Rome and the provincial cities. Docks for unloading ships were built at such places as Ostia and at Porto, where harbours were built by Claudius in A.D. 42 and Trajan in A.D. 103; Trajan's harbour had a hexagonal basin surrounded by warehouses. Private and public warehouses were built for the storage of goods until they could be distributed to the markets. The *Porticus Aemilia*, built alongside the Tiber in Rome, had many vaulted rows opening one into another through a series of arches, the ends of the vaults being left open so that goods could be moved in and out.

Grain was one of the most important imports, and special granaries with double-thickness floors had to be built so that a constant flow of air could provide good ventilation. Oils and wines were kept in great jars set in the ground floor, in a manner similar to those seen on page 34.

In A.D. 79 the eruption of Vesuvius buried the town of Pompeii, and with the silting-up of its port Ostia lost its importance and gradually fell into ruins, and earth eventually buried the remains of its buildings. Excavations have brought both back to light, so that we can once again see what everyday life was like in these places, even down to the personal comments and political slogans (see illustration page 22) painted on the walls.

*Above:* *THERMOPOLIUM, or shop for hot and cold drinks, Via di Diana, Ostia.*
*Below:* *A BAKERY, with mills, at Pompeii*

# WATERWORKS

A good water supply was as much a necessity in ancient times as it is today. To bring water to the cities from the mountain springs, the Romans used their skill as engineers and built aqueducts. These were channels or ducts, lined with a hard waterproof cement, and sometimes covered with slabs of stone, through which the water was conducted down to a reservoir. To cross ravines and rivers the aqueduct was supported on great arches set on piers, sometimes two or even three tiers high. These were built in stone, brick or concrete, whichever materials were most readily available. Where hills were in the way they tunnelled through them. The first aqueduct to bring water to Rome was built in 312 B.C., but by the time of the Emperor Trajan there were eight aqueducts supplying the vast amounts of water required each day. Remains of these great structures may be seen today not only in Rome, but in many parts of the Empire, as well as the remains of bridges which carried their roads, many of which are still in use today.

From the reservoirs the water was fed through pipes, usually of lead, but sometimes of wood or terracotta, to public fountains, where the people had to collect their own supplies. Wealthy men, at their own expense, often laid pipes, stamped with their names, to take water to their own houses, and it was not unknown for

Left: A WATER FOUNTAIN, Pompeii.
Above: PUBLIC LATRINES adjoining the Palaestra, Philippi, Greece, 2nd cent. A.D.

22

*AQUEDUCT, Segovia, Spain, 1st–2nd cent.* A.D.

unscrupulous people to tap the pipes and provide themselves with water without paying for it, although there were strict laws forbidding this sort of thing. Water was also piped to the *thermae*—baths, and special gangs of slaves—*aquarii*—were responsible for maintaining the public services.

The importance of drainage was also realized, and waste water and sewage in Rome were collected in pipes and emptied through a great drain, the *Cloaca Maxima*, into the river Tiber. This semicircular tunnel can still be seen today.

Many people in cities lived in flats—*cenacula*—in tenement blocks—*insulae* (pages 32, 33). Those who lived on the ground floor could have lavatories, but for those who lived above this was not possible, and so the majority of people had to pay to use the public latrines—*foricae*. The seats, with marble tops—in one case in Ostia these were made from old tombstones—were set around the walls of the open room, and beneath them ran a channel of water which carried away the sewage into the main drainage system. There was no privacy, and it was not unusual for people to meet at the *forica* and hold discussions while sitting there.

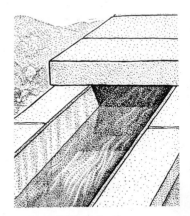

*CONDUIT of the Pont du Gard, Provence, France, 1st cent.* A.D.

23

# BATHS OF CARACALLA

*Rome, early 3rd cent. A.D.*

1. *Reservoirs under*
2. *Stadium* 3. *Libraries
and lecture-rooms* 4. *Shops
and offices* 5. *Calidarium*
6. *Tepidarium* 7. *Ephebeum*
(*see p. 31*) 8. *Frigidarium*

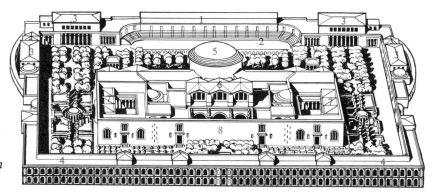

A visit to the *thermae* in the afternoon was part of the social day. In Rome the great bath buildings stood in the *xystus*, a public space filled with trees and shady walks cooled by fountains, where friends could meet and talk. Surrounding this were colonnades and *exedrae*—recesses with seats, libraries and lecture-rooms and a *stadium* for games. From the time of Hadrian mixed bathing was prohibited, men and women bathing at different hours, although in some places separate baths were provided.

After payment of a fee the bathers went to the dressing-rooms—*apodyteria* (page 11), which had shelves around the walls for the storage of clothing. The bathers then went into the *caldarium*, a heated rotunda where they splashed hot water on their bodies, afterwards scraping themselves down with a strigil. Time was then spent in the large vaulted *tepidarium*, a pleasantly warmed hall, before taking a cold plunge in the swimming-bath of the *frigidarium*, often open to the sky as in the picture above.

25

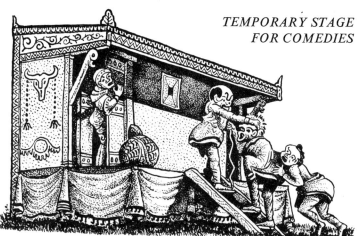

# THE THEATRE
# AND ENTERTAINMENT

The earliest theatrical entertainments in Italy were performed by bands of strolling players, who set up small wooden platforms on which they played to an audience who stood around. The Romans at first forbade the building of stone theatres, perhaps because the presentation of drama and spectacle was associated with politics, and performances were usually given to win the favour of the people. So until the first century B.C., whenever there was a dramatic festival a temporary wooden theatre with a stage and scene building had to be erected which was taken down when the performances were over.

The first permanent stone theatre in Rome, built by Pompey in 55 B.C., was designed with a shrine to the goddess Venus Victrix actually in the auditorium —*cavea*; a flight of steps with seating on either side led up to it. In many ways the Romans copied the theatres of the Greeks, sometimes adapting them and performing plays based on the classical drama of Greece. While the seating in Greek theatres was cut from the face of a hillside, the seats in a Roman auditorium were supported on a series of arches and vaults; this was necessary because much of the land was flat. The shape of the auditorium was semi-circular and the seating enclosed a paved *orchestra*, beyond which was a stage some four or five feet high, backed by a scene building containing dressing-rooms. The front of this building, called the *frons scaenae*, was richly ornamented with marble columns, pediments, niches and statues, and it had from three to five doorways for the actors. The stage was roofed to provide shelter from the sun and rain for the performers, and to protect the decoration and painting on the *frons scaenae*.

The actors performed upon the stage and sometimes in the *orchestra*, but later this area was reserved for special seating for the senators and their wives. The *orchestra* was entered through passageways on either side between the stage and the auditorium, roofed with barrel-vaults with balconies above where

26

the important people who had sponsored the performance and the tribunes and magistrates could sit. The audience reached their seats through arched entrances from the tunnels behind. An open loggia of columns or arches, sometimes with a small shrine or shrines (page 15, caption 3) built into it, ran round the top of the theatre linking the auditorium and stage buildings into one architectural unity; this was called the *porticus*.

Until the performance began the scene was hidden by a curtain—*aulaeum*, which was lowered into a trench at the front of the stage. When the play was over the curtain was raised. Sometimes smaller curtains—*siparia*, could be dropped from the roof of the scene building to hide the *frons scaenae*. Various forms of scenery were used including the *periacti*, a device with three sides which could be pivoted around to show different scenes. A great canvas roof—

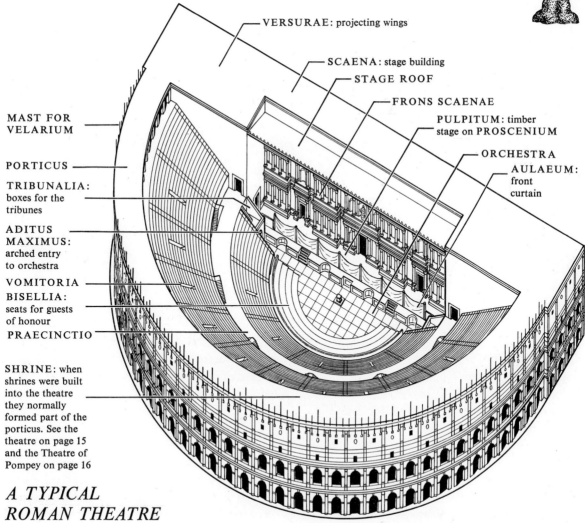

VERSURAE: projecting wings

SCAENA: stage building

STAGE ROOF

FRONS SCAENAE

PULPITUM: timber stage on PROSCENIUM

ORCHESTRA

AULAEUM: front curtain

MAST FOR VELARIUM

PORTICUS

TRIBUNALIA: boxes for the tribunes

ADITUS MAXIMUS: arched entry to orchestra

VOMITORIA

BISELLIA: seats for guests of honour

PRAECINCTIO

SHRINE: when shrines were built into the theatre they normally formed part of the porticus. See the theatre on page 15 and the Theatre of Pompey on page 16

*A TYPICAL ROMAN THEATRE*

*velarium*, which hung from masts around the outside of the theatre, could be drawn across to shelter the audience.

The actors were usually slaves, and although many achieved great fame and fortune they were looked down upon by the free-born Romans. In the early days the character that an actor portrayed was obvious to the audience from the moment he appeared, because of the conventional mask and costume that he wore. Gradually, however, the Romans abandoned the Greek plays and developed their own dramatic entertainments which consisted of mimes and sketches of incidents of everyday life, with a great deal of improvisation. To the delight of the crowd, women took part and the humour was broad and often very vulgar; this type of performance grew out of the work of the strolling players. The place of the classical actor was taken by the *pantomimus*, an actor who interpreted songs and recitations in dance and movement.

Theatres were often used for scenic games

and spectacles. A wall around the edge of the *orchestra* protected the audience from gladiatorial fights and allowed the area to be flooded so that mock sea battles and water sports could take place.

The illustration shows the beginning of a dramatic festival in the theatre at Aspendos, Turkey. A procession of priests is carrying the god's seat from the temple into the *orchestra* where it would be placed to represent his presence during the performance. Only a part of the *aulaeum* has been shown in the raised position, so that you can see the stage; normally this curtain would have extended right across. The drawing of the mask of the tragic actor on the right is from a carving in the theatre at Ostia.

29

*AMPHITHEATRE,*
*Pompeii, 1st cent.* A.D.

Further popular entertainment was provided in great amphitheatres. Emperors desiring to keep the loyalty of the people, and leading citizens anxious to be elected to public office, staged spectacular gladiatorial and wild beast shows. The vast amount of money which was required for the building was considered a necessary expense and amphitheatres were to be found even in small cities. In early times gladiatorial contests had taken place in the *fora*, but the growth of population, and the use of ferocious animals, made this unsuitable.

The seating arrangements were similar to those seen in the theatre, with passageways, ramps and steps beneath the seats, but these completely enclosed an elliptical arena. To prevent the animals from getting too close to the spectators a fence topped with wooden rollers was erected around the arena. The floor of the Flavian amphitheatre, later called the Colosseum (cover and page 17), was constructed of movable wooden sections to allow for the setting-up of scenery, when the arena might perhaps be made to represent a woodland glade in which a hunting scene could be performed. Lifting devices made it possible

*EPHEBEUM AND PERISTYLE, Baths of Diocletian, Rome, early 4th cent. A.D.*

to bring the animals up to the arena at the time when they were required.

Chariot racing at the circus was another favourite entertainment. The best known of these was the *Circus Maximus* (page 16). Tiers of seating surrounded a long rectangle which was rounded at one end. At the other end were the *carceres* where the charioteers and their teams waited for the signal to start which was given by the presiding magistrate. A rope was lowered and the teams raced around the *spina*, a central island on which were statues of gods, shrines and devices for showing the number of laps which had been run: seven wooden eggs on a stand at one end, and seven bronze dolphins at the other. At the height of the Empire the games—*ludi*—lasted several days. There was great excitement amongst the spectators, and many wagers were placed on the outcome of the races.

Like the Greeks the Romans considered that daily physical education was an important part of a young man's upbringing, and it also served as a basis for military training. Gymnasia were attached to the *thermae*, and it was possible to take exercise before bathing. The *ephebeum*, where gymnastic exercises took place, was a covered hall adjoining an open colonnaded court. Wrestlers, whose bodies were covered with oil, took part in contests in the *consistorium*, where special seats were provided for the spectators.

31

# HOUSING

In Rome the continued growth of the population made land expensive, and many people were housed in *insulae*. These blocks of flats faced each other across narrow streets, and greedy landlords, anxious to obtain as much profit as possible, built them several floors high. In many cases they built these blocks of timber framing with an infill of rubble and plaster, a method of construction more suited to

the small houses for which it was generally used, and there are many records of these, often patched-up buildings, crashing to the ground. When built of brick-faced concrete, however, the blocks could be safely built up to the permitted height of sixty-five feet: remains of such buildings may still be seen at Ostia.

These *insulae* were usually built around a central courtyard. In wealthy districts the ground floor was sometimes laid out as a private house—*domus*, an arrangement which

usually commanded a very high rent, but in the poorer areas the ground floor was often divided into shops, with the shopkeeper and his family living on the floor above. The flats on the upper floors were reached by stone staircases leading off the courtyard, and consisted of a number of rooms opening off an inner corridor, leading to a larger room at its end. Sometimes the less desirable residences were shared by more than one family. The windows were not glazed, but could be closed by wooden shutters or curtains, and the only way of heating the premises was by the use of portable stoves (page 38). Furniture consisted only of the barest necessities, which was perhaps fortunate for the inhabitants because fire was a constant danger and families often lost all their possessions. Although some blocks of *insulae* shared a common bathhouse, most of the inhabitants would make use of the great public baths, the luxury of which made up in part for the lack of comfort in their own houses.

The emperors built vast and magnificent palaces; Nero's *Domus Aurea* included lakes, vineyards and woods, as well as a revolving dining-room and walls overlaid with gold and mother-of-pearl. Something of this on a smaller scale can be seen in the remains of a country palace like Hadrian's villa estate at Tivoli, with its lake, colonnades and *nymphaeum*, or shrine of the water nymphs. The remains of Domitian's palace on the Palatine (page 16) give some idea of the grandeur of the many vaulted rooms surrounding the peristyles.

The houses of wealthy citizens were also built around such colonnaded courtyards, and in the country villas there was often a courtyard with ornamental hedges and pools (page 36, caption 1). Many of these homesteads provided a retreat from city life, but others were the bases for local industries, like that at Boscoreale near Pompeii, where the wine and oil grown on the estate were processed and stored ready for sending to the market.

The main living-room of the farmhouse was the kitchen, with a central hearth and a smoke-hole above (pages 2, 3), where the family and servants

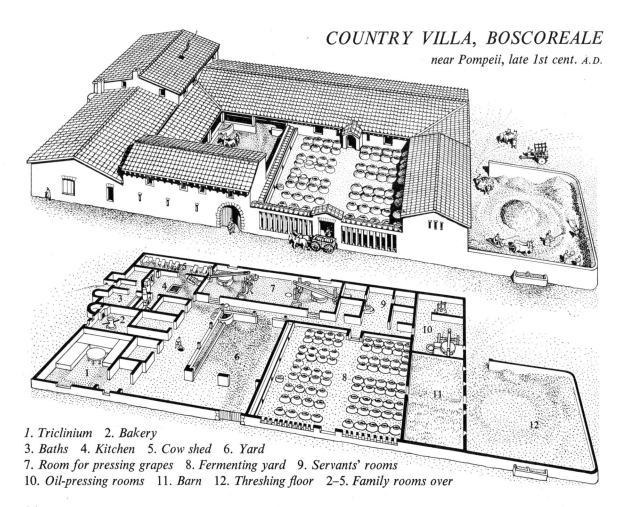

## COUNTRY VILLA, BOSCOREALE

*near Pompeii, late 1st cent.* A.D.

1. *Triclinium*  2. *Bakery*
3. *Baths*  4. *Kitchen*  5. *Cow shed*  6. *Yard*
7. *Room for pressing grapes*  8. *Fermenting yard*  9. *Servants' rooms*
10. *Oil-pressing rooms*  11. *Barn*  12. *Threshing floor*  2–5. *Family rooms over*

Left: *TOWN HOUSE with
shop and workshop at
Caerwent, 1st cent.* A.D.

Below: HYPOCAUST
1. *Marble wall facings*
2. *Mosaic floor on cement*
3. *Bricks on brick piers*
4. *Wall flues*
5. *Hot air from furnaces*

gathered for their meals at separate tables. At Boscoreale, however, there is also a dining-room—*triclinium,* where the master entertained his guests on three couches set around a central table, with food served by the slaves.

Many villas were of the simple corridor type with a row of rooms, sometimes connected by an open verandah. Such villas were often extended with additional rooms at the rear and with flanking wings like those at Frocester, to make the winged corridor plan found also throughout Gaul and Germania.

Most villas of any size had their own bath-house, with dressing-room, cold plunge and furnace. The system used for heating both baths and living-rooms was the hypocaust. The floor was raised on brick pillars to leave a space beneath through which hot air could circulate, and this was carried up the walls in clay flues, the number of which varied with the temperature required. In the better rooms the floors were finished with *tesserae*, small cubes of coloured stones set in a bed of cement. These formed many standard patterns, but a wealthy man would ask the mosaic workers to create a special design. The walls were painted with frescoes, and both these and the mosaics often depicted stories of the gods.

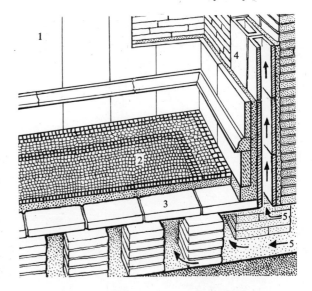

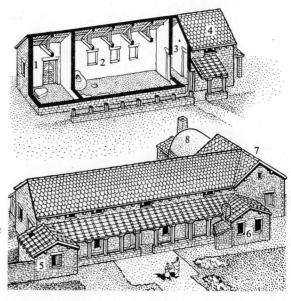

*VILLA, FROCESTER COURT, Glos., Britain.*
*Top: Late 3rd cent.* A.D. *original corridor-type villa.*
1. *Smithy* 2. *Kitchen* 3. *Cross passage* 4. *Master's room*

*Bottom: Late 3rd–mid 4th cent.* AD. *1 and 2 become stable and corn store* 5. *Kitchen* 6. *Master's room with hypocaust* 7. *Cloth workers' room* 8. *Baths*

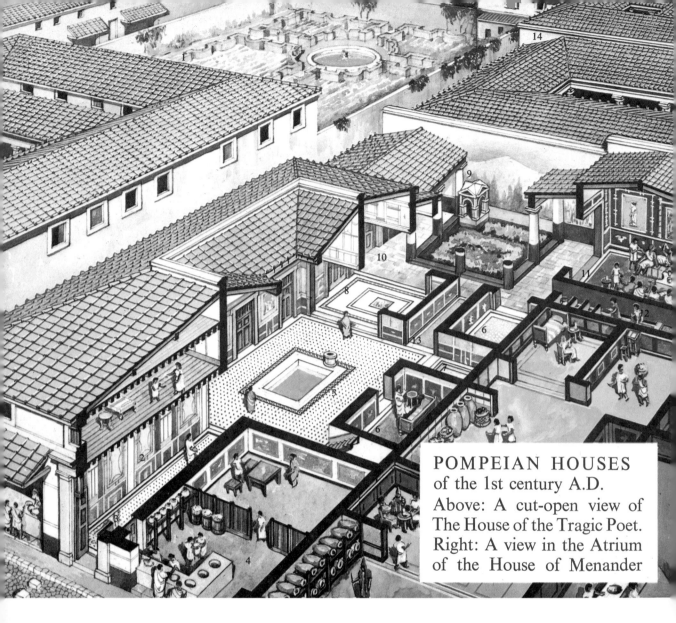

POMPEIAN HOUSES
of the 1st century A.D.
Above: A cut-open view of
The House of the Tragic Poet.
Right: A view in the Atrium
of the House of Menander

1. *House of Pansa* 2. *Fauces*
*—passageway* 3. *Guardian dog*
*mosaic (see p. 38)* 4. *Shop*
5. *Atrium* 6. *Cubiculum*
*—bedroom* 7. *Ala* 8. *Tablinum*
9. *Lararium—shrine* 10. *Peristyle*
11. *Triclinium—dining-room*
12. *Kitchen* 13. *Andron*
14. *Fullonica; a private house*
*used for fulling cloth*

At Pompeii good examples of first century A.D. houses can be seen.
They are entered by a passageway—*fauces*, flanked by rooms
sometimes converted to, or built as, shops; showing a profitable
return for the owner of the house. The *fauces* led directly into the
main living-room, the *atrium*. This had an opening in the roof—
*compluvium*, beneath which was a pool—*impluvium*, which
probably replaced the earlier hearth of this family room, now
removed to a kitchen adjoining the *triclinium*. Next to the
*atrium* and opening into the peristyle was the *tablinum*, where
the master received his guests or studied his books. It could be

1. *Young boar; bronze statue (Naples Museum)* 2. *Market stall of vegetable seller (Ostia Museum)* 3. *Kitchen stove (Naples Museum)* 4. *Guardian dog mosaic from the House of the Tragic Poet* (*see page 36, caption 3*)

closed off with curtains or wooden shutters, when the peristyle could be reached from the *atrium* by a passageway, the *andron. Alae*, open side wings, gave extra space in the *atrium*, and other rooms, usually small and sparsely furnished, were used as bedrooms—*cubicula*. The family shrine was placed either in the atrium itself or in the peristyle.

Much of our knowledge of the way in which the Romans lived has come from their writings, but there are many sculptures, mosaics and paintings which help us to see what they were really like, because the Romans were very naturalistic in their art, portraying people and events exactly as they saw them. The disaster that overtook Pompeii and Herculaneum preserved not only the actual objects, but even the forms of the citizens themselves and their animals, so that we can more clearly visualize the people who created the great buildings whose remains can be seen today.

# ITALIA

Genoa

Perugia

ETRURIA
Tarquinia
ROME
Ostia
Alban Hills

CORSICA

Herculaneum
Pompeii

SARDINIA

MARE ADRIATICUM

MARE
TYRRHENUM

SICILY

Carthage

MARE
IONIUM

Hadrian's Wall
Carrawburgh
Housesteads

York

Chester
Lincoln

Leicester

Caerwent
St. Albans
LONDON
Bath
Silchester

Exeter

# ROMAN BRITAIN

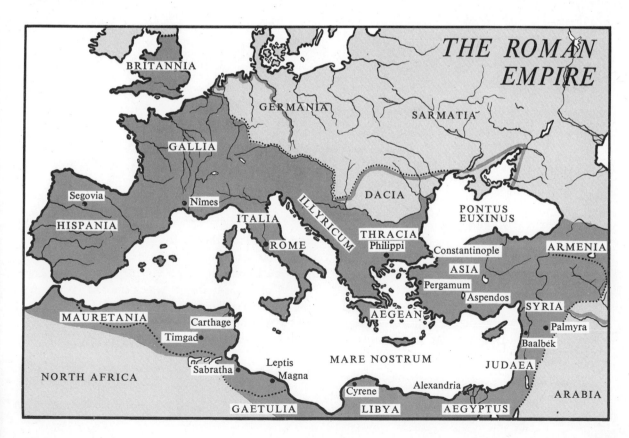

# THE ROMAN EMPIRE

BRITANNIA

GERMANIA

SARMATIA

GALLIA

Segovia

Nimes

DACIA

PONTUS
EUXINUS

HISPANIA

ITALIA

ILLYRICUM

ROME

THRACIA
Philippi

Constantinople

ARMENIA

ASIA
Pergamum
Aspendos

SYRIA
Palmyra
Baalbek

MAURETANIA

Carthage
Timgad

AEGEAN

MARE NOSTRUM

JUDAEA

NORTH AFRICA

Sabratha

Leptis
Magna

Cyrene

Alexandria

ARABIA

GAETULIA

LIBYA

AEGYPTUS

# INDEX

## ACKNOWLEDGMENTS

The authors would like to thank their son, Robert, for his photography of the existing remains of buildings, and his work on the enlargements which formed the basis for many of the reconstructions.

They also wish to thank all those who have given help with criticism and advice, and the many authors whose works or excavation reports have formed the background to this study of Ancient Rome. In particular the drawings on pages 8–9, 16–17 and 24 owe much to information obtained from the great model of Ancient Rome, which may be visited in the Museum of Roman Civilization, E.U.R., Rome, and to which the aerial view on pages 16–17 and the endpapers will provide a most useful key.

## Books by Helen and Richard Leacroft

### THE BUILDINGS OF ANCIENT EGYPT

". . . well written and authoritative and covers much in the way of social history. No other juvenile book covering ancient Egypt gives anything comparable to these informative illustrations. . . . Meets curriculum requests for material on architecture of homes through the ages." *Library Journal*

### THE BUILDINGS OF ANCIENT GREECE

"It could scarcely be better as a library reference for imaginative and recreative work by the pupils." *The Teacher*
"An informative text complements the excellent illustrations on every page which consist of interpretations of Greek life, mostly in color and precise, carefully labelled drawings showing architectural details. Like the Leacrofts' THE BUILDINGS OF ANCIENT EGYPT . . . valuable in the study of a civilization and of architecture in general." *The Booklist (American Library Association)*

### THE BUILDINGS OF ANCIENT ROME

"Should be in every school library, if not in every classroom." *School Librarian*
"It is easy to become absorbed in the past, and the Leacrofts present an enticing opportunity to indulge. The superb illustrations of Roman public and private buildings spark the imagination. They lead one to reconstruct the lives of the people. With scrupulous attention to detail the Leacrofts depict the Romans' technological inventiveness, peerless practicality, and adaptive skill . . . its pages are packed with information." *Christian Teacher*

### THE BUILDINGS OF ANCIENT MAN

"The text . . . is once again interesting and informative and includes clear explanations of many archaeological and technical terms. This would be a good introduction to the subject for people of nine and upwards." *The Times Educational Supplement*
"The text is well written . . . informative illustrations, many of which are in full color . . . this book is excellent for its information on early buildings and their construction." *School Library Journal*

### THE BUILDINGS OF ANCIENT MESOPOTAMIA

". . . The text is clear and efficient. . . . The diagrams are clear, well labelled, and closely fitted to the text. The drawings are also clear and evocative, and the colour spreads are impressive. . . . The publishers must be congratulated on using every square inch of space, end-papers, covers and all, yet without giving the book a cluttered appearance." *The Junior Bookshelf*

ODEUM OF DOMITIAN

PANTHEON

BATHS OF AGRIPPA

THEATRE OF POMPEY

SAEPTA JULIA

TEMPLE OF HADRIAN

THEATRE OF BALBO

TEMPLE OF TRAJAN

TEMPLE OF JUNO MONETA

THEATRE OF MARCELLUS

PORTICUS OCTAVIA

TEMPLE OF JUPITER CAPITOLINUS

TEMPLE OF VENUS GENETRIX

THE CAPITOL

1
2          3
4                6
                    7
5
FORUM OF CAESAR

PONS FABRICUS

FORUM ROMANUM

TIBER

TEMPLE OF AUGUSTUS

9        10      11

PONS AEMILIUS

PALACE OF TIBERIUS

TEMPLE OF FORTUNA VIRILIS

TEMPLE OF CYBELE

HOUSE OF LIVIA

TEMPLE OF PORTUNUS

TEMPLE OF JUPITER VICTOR

PALACE OF DOMITIAN

PALACE OF AUGUSTUS

THE PALATINE

CIRCUS MAXIMUS

STADIUM

PALACE OF SEPTIMUS SEVERUS

BELVEDERE